USBORNE HOTSHOTS

SECRET CODES

D1409047

USBORNE HOTSHOTS

SECRET CODES

Edited by Lisa Miles
Designed by Nigel Reece

Illustrated by Colin King

Series editor: Judy Tatchell
Series designer: Ruth Russell

Additional illustrations by
Guy Smith and Radhi Parekh

Based on material by
Falcon Travis and Judy Hindley

CONTENTS

Codes and ciphers

You can use codes and ciphers to make your letters, diaries and messages impossible to read by people you don't want to read them. Get together with some friends and plan to communicate in code. You can even invent your own codes.

What is a code?

A code is any system of letters, numbers or symbols which can be arranged in a certain way in order to carry information. Every code has a set of rules which allows the message to be read, or decoded, by the person intended to read it.

For instance, these symbols are from a code called pig pen code. See page 24 to find out what they mean.

What is a cipher?

A cipher is a certain type of code which uses the method of substituting or changing around letters or numbers to represent others.

Here is a cipher, known as Code G. See page 8 to find out what it means.

Code book

For every code you use, you need to keep a record of what each letter, number or symbol stands for. Write the rules, or the key, of your code with the uncoded meanings in a code book. Uncoded messages are called plain messages.

If you receive a message without a key, you have to break the code. That is, you have to find out what it means without any clues to help.

Real codes and real spies

For centuries, spies have used codes to communicate. Many of the codes in this book are based on those used by real spies. Translating a message into code is called encoding.

During World War Two, Germany used an electric machine called Enigma to create ciphers. The Enigma codes were almost impossible to break. One of the first ever electronic computers was invented by the British cryptologists (code experts) in order to help them decode Enigma messages.

International spying rose to a height during the Cold War, which lasted from 1945 to the late 1980s. The USA and the Soviet Union employed hundreds of spies to find out about each other's operations.

One of the methods Cold War spies used was passing information on microfilm. Microfilm carries photographs taken with a camera that reduces each photograph to a tiny dot, called a microdot. Microdots can only be read using special magnifying equipment.

> **Pssst! | THE SECRET CODE QUIZ**
>
> Throughout this book, you will see 12 boxes like this. Each one has a code for you to crack. When you have decoded them all, rearrange the sets of words to make a message. The answers are on page 31. No cheating!

Coded messages can be hidden in secret places, like this false pen or the false coin below.

Morse messages

Morse code is a good way to send secret signals. It was invented in 1843 by an American, Samuel Morse. Every letter of the alphabet is replaced by a series of dots and dashes. It was originally used to transmit messages along telegraph wires.

Morse code

One way of using Morse code is to write it down. Here's the alphabet, plus some useful signals.

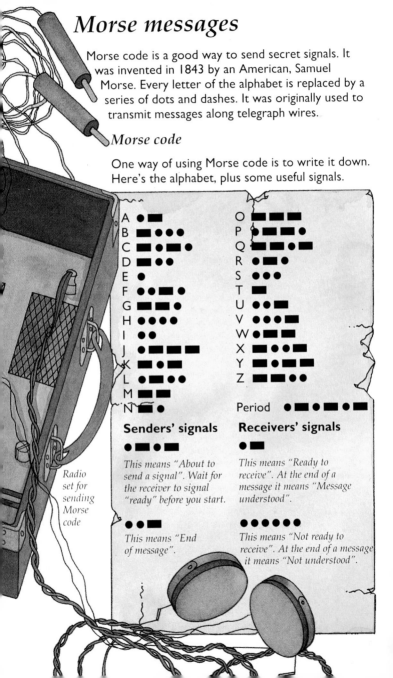

A	●■	O	■■■
B	■●●●	P	●■■●
C	■●■●	Q	■■●■
D	■●●	R	●■●
E	●	S	●●●
F	●●■●	T	■
G	■■●	U	●●■
H	●●●●	V	●●●■
I	●●	W	●■■
J	●■■■	X	■●●■
K	■●■	Y	■●■■
L	●■●●	Z	■■●●
M	■■		
N	■●		

Period ●■●■●■

Radio set for sending Morse code

Senders' signals

●■●■

This means "About to send a signal". Wait for the receiver to signal "ready" before you start.

●●■■

This means "End of message".

Receivers' signals

●■

This means "Ready to receive". At the end of a message it means "Message understood".

●●●●●●

This means "Not ready to receive". At the end of a message it means "Not understood".

Flash dots and dashes

In the dark, you can signal Morse code with flashes from lights. Flash the light for a count of one for a dot and for a count of two for a dash. Here are three ways to signal.

Switch a flashlight on and off to signal.

Flip the edge of a curtain up and down.

Cover the light with a hat to flash a code.

Tapping

During daylight, you could tap out Morse messages. Make two quick taps for a dot and four for a dash.

Tap on water pipes or radiators.

Tap on walls with a pencil.

Tap on railings with a stick.

Wink and blink

Wink to make a dot and blink to make a dash. A stare means the end of a word or a message.

|———— *Wink dot* ————| |———— *Blink dash* ————|

Pssst! | Make this Morse message make sense!

•●■• •■• ●■●■ ●■   ■• • •■■   ■•■■ ■■■ •■• •●■•

Cipher machines

You can create codes using simple machines.

Cipher strip

Draw a strip of 26 boxes. Putting a letter in each box, write out the whole alphabet. Then make a strip of 52 boxes, writing out the whole alphabet twice in a row. Carefully cut out both strips.

Place your shorter "plain" strip so that A is next to F on the long "cipher" strip (see left). In your message, every A in your plain message will be replaced by F in your cipher. Similarly, every B will be replaced by G and so on. This is called Code F. To create different codes, just slide the plain strip along the cipher strip.

Cipher strip, containing two alphabets.

Plain alphabet strip

Keyword scrambler

Here's a way to make lots of different ciphers.

1. Make a chart like the one below, with the plain letters of the alphabet along the top and spaces to write ciphers beneath.

Plain alphabet	ABCDEFGHIJKLMNOPQRSTUVWXYZ
Keyword alphabets	PARISBCDEFGHJKLMNOQTUVWXYZ SPYCLUBADEFGHIJKMNOQRTVWXZ BEWATCHFULDGIJKMNOPQRSVXYZ

2. Choose a word, or a combination of words, that contains all different letters, such as PARIS. This is your keyword.

3. Then fill in the rest of the alphabet, but skip the letters you have already used. This new strip is your cipher.

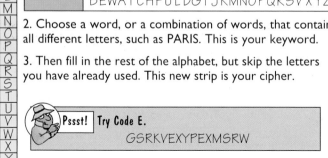

Pssst! Try Code E.

GSRKVEXYPEXMSRW

8

Cipher disk

You can use a disk to create a secret cipher. You turn the disk to match up a code alphabet with a plain alphabet. To make the disk, follow these steps.

The inner disk is the plain alphabet and the outer disk is the cipher. When assembled as shown below, turn the inner disk to change the code.

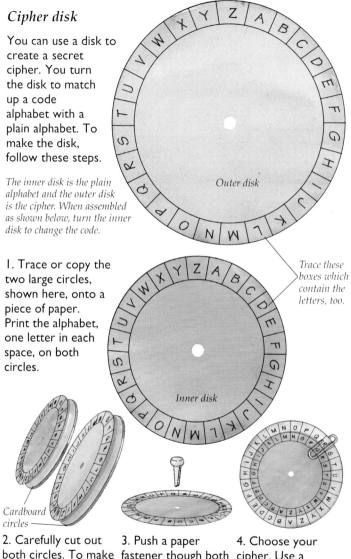

Outer disk

Trace these boxes which contain the letters, too.

1. Trace or copy the two large circles, shown here, onto a piece of paper. Print the alphabet, one letter in each space, on both circles.

Inner disk

Cardboard circles

2. Carefully cut out both circles. To make them more hardwearing, you could attach them to circles of cardboard.

3. Push a paper fastener though both middle dots. Twist it to make a round hole. Bend out the tabs to secure it.

4. Choose your cipher. Use a paperclip to hold the circles in place until you want to change the cipher.

9

Letter grille

Try making this code machine, called a grille, to encode your messages. To read the code, your friend needs to have a grille exactly the same as yours.

How to make the grille

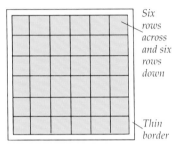

Six rows across and six rows down

Thin border

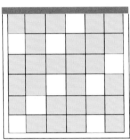

Draw the grid above on a piece of paper. Draw the lines about 2cm (1in) apart. Draw a thin border and cut around the outside edge.

Shade in the top edge only of the border with a red felt-tip pen. Carefully cut out the unshaded squares above.

Encoding the message

To encode the message "This is how to use the secret code grille", follow the steps from 1 to 5.

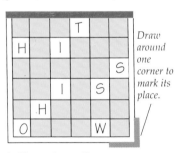

Draw around one corner to mark its place.

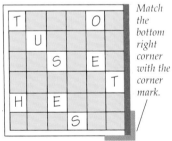

Match the bottom right corner with the corner mark.

1. Place the grille on some paper and print one letter of the message in each space, from left to right, starting at the top.

2. Give the grille one turn clockwise so that the red edge lies on the right. Fill the spaces with the next set of letters.

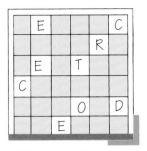

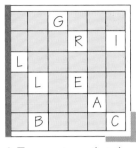

3. Turn the grille again so that the red edge lies along the bottom. Match the corner up and fill the spaces with the next set of letters.

4. Turn again so that the red edge lies on the left. Fill in the rest of the message. There will be three spare spaces. Fill in these with the first three letters of the alphabet.

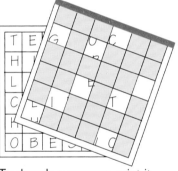

5. Lift the grille and you will see the grid of letters above. To complete the code, write the letters out in a long line, like this: *Tegtoc huirri lestes cliest hheoad obeswc.*

To decode a message, print it from left to right across a blank grid. Place the grille over the message with the red edge at the top. Turn it to show all the letters in turn.

 Pssst! **Use the grille to decode this message:**

BBKULC SIBLDM NESFHO GORPNI NEGHQI
PRJAUS

Body language

You can give people signs by the way that you stand or move. Here are some simple body language codes that you can use if you want to pass a message to a friend from a distance or across a crowded room.

Face code

Use your first finger to point to different parts of your face. Each position is a code for a different message. Rest your head on your hand and sit still to indicate to your friend that you are ready to start passing a secret signal.

Danger

Keep away

Meet me later

Go to headquarters

End of message

Follow me

Clothing codes

You can also use clothing and accessories to signal silently across a room. For instance, a handkerchief in the pocket might mean "meet today as agreed". No handkerchief might mean "no meeting". Pencils in a breast pocket could give information about what time to meet.

A blue pencil in the middle could be the code for 2pm.

Hand and leg code

You can send quick messages and warnings with your hand and leg positions too.

Signal: *One hand in pocket.*
Message: *Yes*

Signal: *Two hands in pockets.*
Message: *No*

Signal: *Both hands behind back.*
Message: *No message*

Signal: *Scratching ear.*
Message: *I'll phone later.*

Signal: *Standing on one leg.*
Message: *I'm going home.*

Signal: *Scratching head.*
Message: *Meet as agreed.*

Signal: *Scratching back of neck.*
Message: *Careful! You are being watched.*

Signal: *Crossing one leg over the other.*
Message: *Message at the hiding place.*

Pssst!

What does my body language say?

Sign language

Try communicating in secret by using sign language.

Pssst! Read this word.

Finger spelling

You can spell out words using signs to represent letters. With practice you can sign fairly quickly. People who don't know sign language won't be able to understand you.

A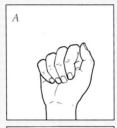

B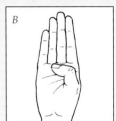

C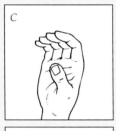

D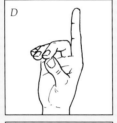

E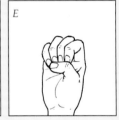

F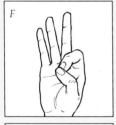

G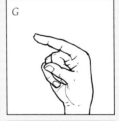

H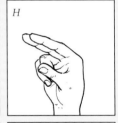

I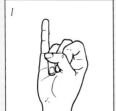

J

K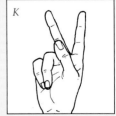

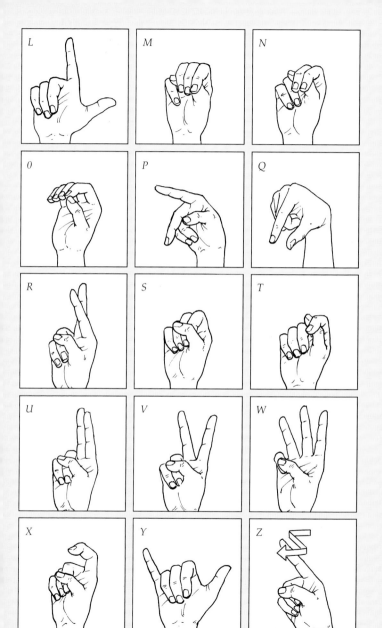

15

Signing words

As well as finger spelling, you can also use signs for individual words. This will make it even quicker for you to communicate in signs. Here are some, based on a sign language for the deaf. The arrows show how to move your hands to do the sign.

Pssst!

What does the sign say?

Yes

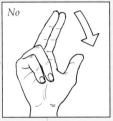
No

Again

Excellent

Good

Bad

Numbers

Here are the numbers in sign language.

1

2

3

4

5

6

7

8

9

10

16

Name

Start

Go

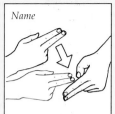
Finish

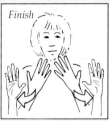
Meet

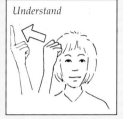
Understand

Please

Thank you

Don't know

Indian sign language

Years ago, many different tribes of North American Indians lived across the continent. They all spoke different languages, so many of them also used a sign language that could be understood by different tribes.

Arrow

Buffalo

Friend

Horse

Indian

Peace

Trade

Tepee

Invisible inks

To make sure your codes definitely don't get read by the wrong person, you can write them in invisible ink.

Potato ink

1. Make a pen by sharpening one end of a used match with a piece of sandpaper or a nail file.

2. Hold a potato, as shown, and cut off both ends with a knife. Be very careful as you do this.

3. Stand the potato on one end. Scoop a fairly deep hole in the top of it with a spoon.

4. Use the blade of the knife to scrape and squeeze the juice from the top of the potato into the hole.

5. Dip your "pen" into the ink and write with it. When the ink dries, it will be invisible.

6. For the message to appear, put it into a cool oven (250°F, 120°C, Gas Mark 2) for 15 minutes.

Water writing

Wet some paper thoroughly. Lay it on a smooth, hard surface. Cover it with dry paper and write with a pen. Hold the wet paper to the light to see the message.

When it dries, the message will vanish. To make it reappear, wet it again with a paintbrush. To make the message permanent, brush it with watery paint.

Letter clue

You can write invisible messages on the back of an ordinary letter, or between the lines or down its sides. So that your friend can read the secret message, give him or her a clue to show what kind of ink you have used and where you have written the message.

For instance, use the address code as your clue. <u>WS</u> might mean that a <u>W</u>ater message has been written down the <u>S</u>ide of the paper. In the picture below, <u>PJB</u> means that a <u>P</u>otato <u>J</u>uice message has been written along the <u>B</u>ottom.

Address code giving a clue to the secret message. You can also use lemon juice, milk, onion juice or cola as inks.

HOTSHOTS
SPYCATCHER'S CLUB
BOX <u>PJB</u>123

DEAR L,

THE TRAIN LEAVES TONIGHT.
MEET ME AT EIGHT. BE SURE
TO BRING YOUR TEDDY.

WITH LOVE,
N

XXXX

Pssst!

Decode this potato juice writing. Find out how on page 24.

19

Puzzles in print

Use a book, newspaper or comic to pass secret codes to your friends. You could leave books or newspapers on a bench, where they can be picked up.

Crossword messages

Most newspapers and magazines have crosswords. Fill in the blank squares with your message, by writing down in columns. Fill in spare squares with other letters. No one looks at finished crosswords, so this is a good way to pass messages.

Book code

Use the words inside a book to make a secret message.

Look at the code sheet on the far right. In each set of three numbers, the first stands for a page number, the second for a line number and the third is the number of words along the line.

You could use this method to send a message to a friend by lending her a book.

CHAPTER THREE

THE GOLD MINERS' RETURN

It had been a long, hard hike walking back down Johnson's Mountain. The mules were heavily loaded up with equipment and the precious pieces of gold that the miners had found. Harry, Jim and Charles were exhausted after spending all summer at the gold mine.

Keep the book and the code sheet separate, so the key to the code doesn't fall into the wrong hands!

Pin-hole messages

On the front of every newspaper is its date. Prick a small hole with a pin over one number of the date. This number tells what page the message is on.

Turn to that page. Use the pin to prick holes in a row, above letters that spell out a message. At the end, prick a hole in a space between words.

To read the message, fold the newspaper so that the message page has no other pages behind it. Hold it up to the light. You can then see the pin holes.

It had been back-breaking work. Now they were on their way home to stay with their families until the spring.

Suddenly, they heard a whooping noise behind them. Bandits – five of them on horseback! Harry grabbed his gun and yelled to the others, "We're gonna have to fight for it lads. Quick!"

(41)

Code sheet

Use this code sheet to figure out a hidden message. Don't count headings as a line.

41.3.3
40.4.3
40.7.2
41.4.1
41.7.2

The answer is on page 30.

Pssst!

Use the pages of this book to crack this code.

5.5.7
20. 4.1

Secret diary

Keep your diary secret from prying eyes by writing it in code. Here's how.

Dot code messages

Write a boring entry in your diary, such as how you spent the evening watching TV. Then you can write in dot code what you really want to say.

Drawing the code

Make an alphabet strip that fits the width of the pages of your diary. To make the code extra hard to break, you could scramble the letters of the alphabet into a different order.

1. Hold the strip to line up with the left-hand side of the page. Start near the top of the page and put a dot over the first letter of whatever it is you want to say.

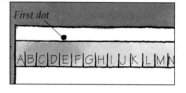

2. Move the strip down slightly and put a second dot over the second letter. Continue moving the strip down to make each new dot until you have completed the message.

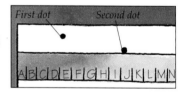

If your message is a short one, you could disguise the dots as pictures underneath a normal diary entry.

In this picture, the dots have been turned into birds.

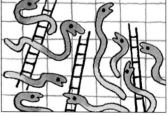

On this picture of a game, the snakes' eyes are the dots.

Scrambled secrets

Scramble your diary's secrets with this code machine. Write out numbers on a strip of paper, from 1 to 10.

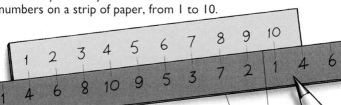

Then write out the numbers 1 to 10 in random order. Repeat them in exactly the same order again, so that you now have a strip of paper with 20 numbers on.

Original line number

Coded line number

Divide the page into 10 lines. Then move the original strip so that 1 lines up with another number, for instance 4, on the code strip. Write the first line of your diary on line 4, the second on line 6 and so on. Remember which number you started with so that you can decode your diary.

chair and she had sat on it.

someone had spilled paint on her

should be so furious.

Monday May 8. Today, our

We couldn't think why she

teacher stormed into the

Then we discovered that

class. She said she was

into her office one by one.

calling all kids

Pssst!
Using the code above, find original line 4 in this diary.

Pig pen code

In this code, a different symbol stands for each
letter of the alphabet. At the end of each word,
leave a space. The person decoding the message
can then form the words into sentences.

Making the code

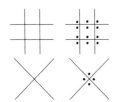

A B C
D E F
G H I

J K L
M N O
P Q R

SECRET

1. To make the key
for pig pen code,
start by drawing the
four patterns shown
above. These will be
broken down into
single shapes later.

2. Now write in the
letters of the
alphabet like this.
The pattern of lines
and dots next to
each letter is used
as its code.

3. This example
shows how pig pen
code can be used to
represent the word
"secret". Now write
your own message
in pig pen code.

Here's the full alphabet.

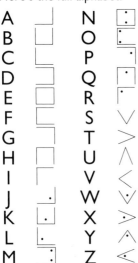

A	N
B	O
C	P
D	Q
E	R
F	S
G	T
H	U
I	V
J	W
K	X
L	Y
M	Z

Pssst! What does this say
in pig pen code?

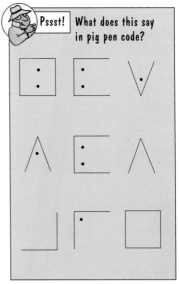

Symbol shape puzzle

Here is a tricky code that is based on symbols and shapes. Can you figure it out? Read each of the five strips from left to right. There is an extra clue at the bottom of the page if you need it.

Invent your own symbol code

You could invent your own symbol code based on a kind of picture writing. Use simplified shapes that show what each symbol means, but which don't make it too obvious.

Can you guess what the message in the box might mean? The answer is on page 30.

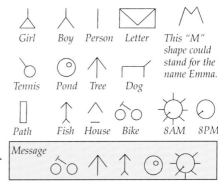

Girl   *Boy*   *Person*   *Letter*   This "M" shape could stand for the name Emma.

Tennis   *Pond*   *Tree*   *Dog*

Path   *Fish*   *House*   *Bike*   *8AM*   *8PM*

Message

Clue: This code is similar to pig pen code – look at the shapes.

Quick codes

Here are some quick codes. Photocopy the chart below, so that you have a quick decoding device.

Angle code

An angle shape is numbered 1-7 for the first seven letters of the alphabet. Its position is then changed and numbered from 1-7 and so on until the end of the alphabet.

Semaphore

This code is usually signaled by holding flags at arms' length. Here, the same positions are used, but the code is written like the hands of a clock.

Pssst! Decode these semaphore symbols:

Decoding chart

Plain	Angle	Semaphore
A	1	
B	2	
C	3	
D	4	
E	5	
F	6	
G	7	
H	1	
I	2	
J	3	
K	4	
L	5	
M	6	
N	7	
O	1	
P	2	
Q	3	
R	4	
S	5	
T	6	
U	7	
V	1	
W	2	
X	3	
Y	4	
Z	5	

More quick codes

There are hundreds of different ways to make codes, simply by rearranging letters.

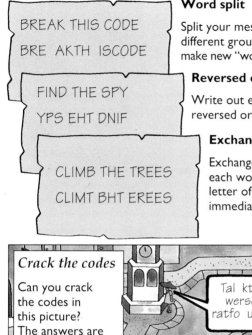

BREAK THIS CODE

BRE AKTH ISCODE

Word split

Split your message into different groups of letters to make new "words".

FIND THE SPY

YPS EHT DNIF

Reversed order

Write out each sentence in reversed order.

Exchange letters

CLIMB THE TREES

CLIMT BHT EREES

Exchange the last letter of each word with the first letter of the word that immediately follows it.

Crack the codes

Can you crack the codes in this picture? The answers are on page 30.

Tal ktoflo werselle ratfo untain

Rewot kcolc ta tah der ni lrig teem

Thm eessagi ei snsidt ehb elub eook

Hiding secret messages

Once you have written your secret message in code, you might need to hide it somewhere, where you or someone else can pick it up again later. Here are some crafty hiding places.

False sole

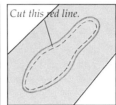

Cut this red line.

1. Put your shoe on a piece of light cardboard and draw around it.

2. Cut just inside this line to make a false sole that will fit inside your shoe.

3. Slip the message between the real sole and the false sole as shown.

In the park

Parks or gardens are good for finding lots of secret hiding places. Here are some. (Tell an adult where you are going before you set out.) Remember not to make it look as though you are hiding or collecting anything.

Before you go out, put a message in a bottle. If you see a rabbit hole, slip the bottle inside it.

Pssst!

Decode this. (No clues for this one!)

SREKCARC EDOC

Leave a newspaper on a bench with a message inside it.

Secret pocket

Make two tabs with some tape.

1. Cut off the corner of an unused tea bag and empty out the tea.

Secret message

2. Tuck the message inside the tea bag. Stick it inside your sleeve.

Pen message

Message

1. Roll up the message tightly and keep it in the top of a pen.

Message

2. Or, unscrew an ink pen and wrap the paper around the cartridge.

Hole in the wall

1. Roll up the message tightly and tie a piece of thread or string around it.

2. Hide it in a crack in a wall. Use the string to pull it out again.

Pretend to smell some flowers. Push a bottle containing a message into the soil.

Kneel by a tree and pretend to tie your shoelace. Hide the message under a tree root.

Pretend to bang your toe against a log. Bend down to rub it and hide the message under the log.

Sit down on a bench and pin a message with a drawing pin underneath the bench.

Answers

Page 4

The pig pen code says: Crafty Code.
The cipher code says: Secret Cipher.

Page 21

Find the coded message by using the code sheet as a key to locate
the position of the code words.

Page 25 – Symbol shape puzzle

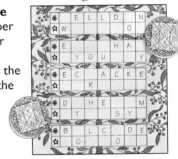

The key to the symbols in the upper
rows of each strip lie in the flower
grid (top right). The key to the
symbols in the bottom rows lie in the
star grid (bottom left). Match up the
symbols to the shapes
surrounding the letters on the
grids. They say: Well done. You
have cracked the symbol code.

Page 25 – Symbol code

The message reads: Cycle to the tree near the fishpond at 8am.

Page 27

1. The letters have been split into different groups. The message
   says: Talk to flower seller at fountain.
2. The sentence is written in reverse order. It says: Meet girl in
   red hat at clock tower.
3. The last and first letters of each word are exchanged. The
   message says: The message is inside the blue book.

Pssst! ANSWERS TO THE SECRET CODE QUIZ

Page 7
Use the patterns of dots and dashes on page 6 to read:
FROM NEW YORK

Page 8
Use the code strip along the left hand edge of page 8 to read off Code E. It reads:
CONGRATULATIONS

Page 11
Turn the letter grille to reveal:
USBORNE PUBLISHING

Page 13
Find the matching spy on page 12. He is signaling the words:
END OF MESSAGE

Page 14
Find the matching pictures to spell:
FROM

Page 16
Find the matching picture. It represents the word:
EXCELLENT

Page 19
Use pig pen code on page 24 to spell:
PARIS

Page 21
Look for page 5, line 5, word 7 and page 20, line 4, word 1 to find:
THE MOST

Page 23
Find 4 on the strip of original line numbers. Read off the new line number on the code strip. The line is:
CALLING ALL KIDS

Page 24
Translate the pig pen code to reveal the words:
NOW YOU ARE

Page 26
Translate the semaphore code to reveal the words:
TO LONDON TO

Page 28
Read the words from back to front. They read:
CODE CRACKERS

Unscramble the sets of words into order to find an answer:

CALLING ALL KIDS FROM NEW YORK TO LONDON TO PARIS.
CONGRATULATIONS FROM USBORNE PUBLISHING. NOW YOU ARE THE
MOST EXCELLENT CODE CRACKERS. END OF MESSAGE.
Did you get something like this?!

Tips for code breakers

1. Test your skill and keep in practice by exchanging coded messages with your friends. At first, you could give each other clues to the codes you have used.

2. When decoding a message, write it in large capital letters with plenty of space below each line. When you find the plain letter meaning of a code letter, write it under each one throughout the message, like this.

Code message

UIF DBU TBU PO UIF NBU
T   T   T   T   T —— *U stands for T in the plain message*

3. Try to find vowels (AEIOU and also Y) because every word has at least one. Look for single letter words – these will be "I" or "A".

4. Note patterns of double or repeated letters. OO, EE and TH are very common. Look for words that have recognizable patterns, like these.

CHurCH   TomORROw   lETTEr

5. Codes do not usually include punctuation marks, because it helps the code breaker to crack them. So, as you decode a message, try to break it into phrases as you go along.

6. Doing crosswords and playing word games are good practice for code breaking. They give you a feel for letter patterns and how words work together.

Index

This book includes material previously published in *The Rainy Day Book, Codes and Ciphers, Secret Messages* and *The Knowhow Book of Spycraft*. First published in 1996 by Usborne Publishing Ltd, Usborne House, 83-85 Saffron Hill, London, EC1N 8RT, England.
Copyright © Usborne Publishing Ltd 1997, 1994, 1978, 1975
Frist published in America March 1997 AE